T0128787

OOPS
I DID IT AGAIN

GOD HATES SIN, BUT HE LOVES YOU

RON KELLY

AuthorHouse™
1663 Liberty Drive
Bloomington, IN 47403
www.authorhouse.com
Phone: 1-800-839-8640

Published by AuthorHouse 7/16/2012

ISBN: 978-1-4772-4008-3 (sc)
ISBN: 978-1-4772-4009-0 (e)

Library of Congress Control Number: 2012912249

Acknowledgements

First and foremost, I give thanks to my Lord and Savior, Jesus Christ, who is the author and finisher of my faith. Philippians 4:13 is etched into my spirit: "For I can do all things through Christ which strengthens me." I thank God as He continues to provide me with the wisdom necessary to do a great work in His Kingdom.

To my wife, Kelsey, thank you for the love and support you've shown me throughout this journey. To my New Generation Christian Center family, I always feel your love, support, encouragement and prayers. Special thanks to my editors, Theresa and Grace, as well as all the professionals at Author House Publishing.

Finally, to all of you who will read this book. I pray that you find liberation through the sacrifice of what Jesus did for you on that ole rugged cross. He loves you unconditionally, even when you find yourself saying, "Oops, I Did It Again!"

Contents

Introduction. ix

Prologue: The Sermon behind the Book. xv
Sermon Title: "Oops, I Did It Again!"

Chapter 1:   Just Forget About It 1

Chapter 2:   Stop Faking It 9

Chapter 3:   His Grace and Mercy 21

Chapter 4:   A God of a ~~Second~~ Another Chance 29

Chapter 5:   You Must Be Born Again! 39

Epilogue: Be Encouraged. 49

Introduction

Several months ago, while getting some work done at Panera Bread Company, which I jokingly refer to as my second office; I happened to overhear a conversation among two young women and a young man. They were hanging out, joking around and discussing life. As usual, I had several books spread across the table, including my Bible. As I pecked around on my laptop and sipped on my coffee, I wasn't particularly tuned in to these young people's conversation. That was until I heard one of the young ladies say:

"I'm really getting turned off by the whole 'church' thing. I've been going to church all my life, but I just can't seem to get it right! I'm really starting to think religion is not for me."

As soon as I heard this statement, I immediately stopped what I was doing and focused my attention on their conversation. As I listened in, I tried to remain inconspicuous so they would continue their candid chat.

The young man then said, "Whatever! You couldn't stop

going to church even if you wanted to! Your whole family is a bunch of holy rollers!"

"Yeah, that's one of the main reasons I'm thinking about quitting. I'm always being compared to them, and I don't even come close to measuring up!" she replied.

The other young lady chimed in, "I feel the same way whenever I go to my church. It seems like everybody there has it all together and can see right through me with their spiritual bifocals! My life is not as raggedy as those of most people my age, but I always feel guilty and ashamed whenever I get around church folks!"

The gentleman responded, "I know what I believe, but I don't think I'll ever walk or talk like the people at my church. They're just too holy for me!"

The first young lady added, "Maybe we'll grow into it later on in life. They said my uncle was a hell raiser, but now he's a preacher!"

The three of them laughed off their casual conversation, refilled their coffee and moved on to the next topic of discussion. I nearly held my peace and let them continue their casual lunch, but I couldn't resist the opportunity to witness to them. On this particular day, I happened to be wearing a sweat suit, ball cap and Jordan tennis shoes, not looking at all the part of a minister. I know now that it was my attire that made me seem approachable to these young people.

I introduced myself to them as a minister and apologized for eavesdropping. I then asked if I could talk to them about their previous conversation. They invited me to join them, and for the next hour, we had a wonderful and fulfilling discussion about Christianity. They were like sponges, soaking up what God had placed on my heart to share with them. These bright twenty-somethings asked a plethora of faith-based questions. At times, I even felt comfortable enough to let down my guard and share examples of the inconsistencies and flawed behavior that plagued me even after I became a minister.

As we talked, it became apparent to me that no one had ever really told them the true meaning of Christianity. I explained to them that contrary to popular belief, even the best Christians struggle with sin. From time to time, all Christians stumble during their journey. As our coffee turned cold, God used me to encourage these three strangers to take another look at Christianity. There was no need for them to renew their *religion*; they only needed to reestablish their *relationship* with a Savior who paid it all!

Meeting these young people at Panera that day was no chance encounter. In fact, my visit with them confirmed something I had been feeling for years: Christianity has a serious image problem! Millions of people are straying from the faith, because they are frustrated at their inability to measure up and be who or what society says they should be.

I've had spiritual moments when it felt like my sin had gotten the best of me, and like many of you, I've been in a terrible place where I convinced myself that I could never measure up. There was a period in my Christian life when I embraced my fallible lifestyle and even accepted the fact that I was stuck forever in this place called spiritual mediocrity. I will even admit that after being called into the ministry, I have had guilty moments that left me feeling hopeless.

I wrote this book for Christians who just can't seem to get it together. This book is for all Christians who have set the bar for themselves so high that they continually fall short and miss the mark. This book was written for Christians from all walks of life who do things they regret – Christians who struggle, Christians with problems and Christians with issues.

It is truly a trick of the enemy to keep you in bondage and perpetually haunted by your personal inconsistencies, doubts, failures, addictions and mishaps. My desire is to help you realize and understand: It doesn't matter what you've done; you don't have to remain in bondage for that sin, because Jesus has set the captives free from sin and condemnation to live in the liberty that only His love can bring (Luke 4:18).

There is no reason for you to continue in bondage as a slave to sin. There is also no reason for you to continue to live in the shadows of denial and the concealment of sin. Jesus said in John 8:32-36, "*And you shall know the truth, and the truth shall make you free.*" *They answered Him, "We are Abraham's descendants, and have never been in bondage to anyone. How can You say, 'You will be made free'?" Jesus answered them, "Most assuredly, I say to you, whoever commits sin is a slave of sin. And a slave does not abide in the house forever, but a son abides forever. Therefore if the Son makes you free, you shall be free indeed.*"

We often forget that Jesus surrounded himself around misfits, lepers and sinners. Well, you and I are no different than the men and women of yesterday. If you want to find Jesus, you don't have to look very far. You can find Him in the midst of incompetent religious leaders, burnt-out believers and moral misfits.

In other words, Jesus can still be found among the people whose lives are far from perfect. The Lord will never shun you away, so don't allow society or the local church make you feel as if you are not good enough. Jesus wants you to run to Him, not away from Him. He will meet you right where you are, at this very moment in your life. Open your eyes to the fullness of His love as He transforms you with His Grace and Mercy.

Stop trying to convince yourselves that you will come to Jesus after you've cleaned up your act. The truth is, that will never happen because you can't fix yourself! We're all going to occasionally miss the mark now and then. However, true spirituality is for imperfect people willing to let God turn their messes into masterpieces, believing that our messes are God's opportunities.

It's time to remove the shackles of guilt and shame. My goal is to provide you with a practical approach to dealing with day-to-day disappointments and shortcomings. I am convinced that genuine faith begins with admitting that we will never really have it all together. That being said, I am in no way suggesting that we have a license to sin. I wrote this book to help you understand that even though you are flawed with imperfections, God thinks you're beautiful, and He loves you unconditionally!

In the following pages you will discover personal testimonies and scriptural references that provide a roadmap back to a fulfilling relationship with our Lord and Savior, Jesus Christ. As you trek through the pages of this book, I invite you to open your eyes to a deeper level of spirituality and allow yourself to be unconditionally loved by our Heavenly

Father, who meets you and transforms you in the midst of an imperfect and unpredictable life!

The chapters are short, precise and filled with a wealth of information. Therefore, I encourage you to read this book with a highlighter and pen. Take notes as you read, making this your personal resource manual for future reference. Meditate and pray between the chapters, asking God to open your heart and give you an understanding that will speak directly to you.

Prologue:

The Sermon behind the Book

Delivered at New Generation Christian Center

February 5, 2006

Romans 7:18-20, *And I know that nothing good lives in me, that is, in my sinful nature. I want to do what is right, but I can't. I want to do what is good, but I don't. I don't want to do what is wrong, but I do it anyway. But if I do what I don't want to do, I am not really the one doing wrong; it is sin living in me that does it.*

Sermon Title: "Oops, I Did It Again!"

I think it would be safe to say we've all had moments where we've become disappointed with ourselves, moments where we've become frustrated at our inability to resist sin. As Christians, we strive to live a positive and productive life, but it often seems that no matter how hard we try to do the right thing, evil is always present. When we miss the mark and succumb to the temptations that we know are contrary to the word of God, we are left with a feeling of disappointment in ourselves.

Dealing with self-disappointment is an ongoing private war. There's an internal struggle going on that's not seen by others as we fail to do that which we know we ought to do. Unless we tell someone (other than God) the only person who knows about our self-disappointment is the man or the woman who stares back at us in the mirror.

Our reflection in the mirror reminds us of everything we promised ourselves we would be and holds us accountable to what we are doing to make good on those promises. In other words, the man or woman that we see in the mirror will expose the size of the gap between our ideals and our reality! It doesn't matter who you are; this reality can be incredibly disappointing.

Unfortunately, many people today view life as a game, because we get caught up in the thrills and the excitement that life brings. However, once we've done something that conflicts with our spirits, the dust will settle and the smoke will clear, leaving us reeking with guilt, shame and disappointment. Our knee-jerk decisions will cause us to stoop to a level in life that is not only embarrassing, but will often hurt other people in the process.

Everybody knows who Britney Spears is, right? Well, back in May of 2000, she released her sophomore album, "Oops!...I Did It Again." The album became a commercial success after debuting at the top position on the U.S. Billboard, selling over 1.3 million units during its first week. The album produced three worldwide hits, but the most popular was the lead single, "Oops!...I Did It Again."

For those of you who aren't familiar with this song, allow me to enlighten you. It's a song about a young lady who enjoys teasing this young man in a way that leads him on. She thinks it's a game, and she enjoys playing the game, suggesting that her intent was never to do him any harm. However, when she realizes that she breaks this young man's heart, she brushes it off by saying, "Oops!...I Did It Again!"

Just like Britney Spears, many of us will flirt with fire and then brush off our disappointments by saying, "Oops, I did it again!" We light up another cigarette after telling ourselves the last one was the last one. "Oops, I did it again!" We cheated on our spouses when we took a vow to remain faithful. "Oops, I did it again!" We lost our temper when we promised ourselves we would be in control. "Oops, I did it again!" We lied when we promised ourselves we would be truthful and honest. "Oops, I did it again!" We had too much to drink, we're looking at pornographic content on the internet or we gambled away the rent money at the casino. "Oops, I did it again!"

As Christians, we struggle daily with self-disappointment. Our only redeeming grace is to know that while the God in whom we serve is not happy with our personal failures, He is still forgiving and merciful! I know this is a hard concept for many of you to wrap your head around, but here's the reality: Despite our flaws, short-comings and general ugliness, God still loves us unconditionally! God hates sin, but He doesn't hate the person who commits the sin! God hates the lie, but He doesn't hate the person who tells the lie! God hates the crime, but He doesn't hate the criminal! In other words, God may hate what you've done, but He doesn't hate you!

It doesn't matter what you've done or how many times you've said, "Oops, I did it again!" 1 John 1:9 says, *"If we confess our sins, He is faithful and just to forgive us for our sins, and to cleanse us from all unrighteousness.*" Now I don't know about you, but that's a reason to give Him praise in this place. What an awesome Savior!

As we look at our text this morning, it focuses on Paul as he explains the nature of the believer's life in Christ as opposed to the law. In general, the book of Romans focuses on the believer's sanctification, but here, we see Paul's personal struggle to perfect himself and become closer to God. We know from Bible history that at one point, Paul fought against the advancement of the church, but once he gave his life over to God, his battle shifted!

Paul went from opposing God's laws to one who was a true believer, but like many of us, he also struggled to measure up to God's expectations. Paul wants to do the right thing in his heart. The "spirit" man within him wants to go right and avoid what the law calls sin. However, the "carnal" man within him wants to go left and rebel against his spiritual side. Paul is literally going through a spiritual tug-of-war!

Our spirit has been set apart by God, but our minds continue to have the pattern of that old way of thinking. Although our spirit is secure in Christ, there's still a battle going on with our mind, wills and emotions. Our desire is to do the right thing and leave that old pattern of living in the past. We want to embrace our new life in Christ, but our flesh is saying, "Wait a minute. I didn't sign up for this!" How many of you know today that sin will take advantage of your flesh every time? Sin will pervert the law in order to entice us. Paul couldn't control the sin within himself. It caused him to do the things he didn't want to do again and again, making Paul a wretched man indeed.

Ninety-eight percent of today's text describes Paul's struggles with sin, but instead of being depressed by this passage, we should be encouraged, because Paul faced the same daily struggles with his flesh that you and I struggle with today, yet God still used Paul in a mighty way. The remaining two percent of the text gives us the answer we need to overcome our tendencies to sin.

In the first seven verses, Paul describes the Christian's fight against the flesh. And as Christians, we should be able to relate to what Paul is saying here. Paul makes the issue of his sin problem crystal clear. He's not speaking hyperbole (overstating or exaggerating) just to make a point. This thing was real to Paul. He was locked into an all-out war between his flesh and his spirit.

Listen to the text again (Romans 7:18-20) *"And I know that nothing good lives in me, that is, in my sinful nature. I want to do what is right, but I can't. I want to do what is good, but I don't. I don't want to do what is wrong, but I do it anyway. But if I do what I don't want to do, I am not really the one doing wrong; it is sin living in me that does it."*

Paul was describing the inner turmoil of the Christian walk, where the good and bad natures are always at odds. But even though Paul was disappointed with himself, he still saw an opportunity for victory in Jesus Christ. Paul said that we all delight in the law of God after the inward man, yet the problem is we also have the law of sin in our members as well. Romans 7:23, *"But I see another law in my members, warring against the law of my mind, and bringing me into captivity to the law of sin which is in my members."*

And so, even though God doesn't grade sin, we have a natural human tendency to do so. But Jesus said He forgives all manner of sin, which provides the answer to Paul's question in the following verse (24) when he said, *"O wretched man that I am! Who will free me from this life that is dominated by sin and death?"* He answers his own question in the final verse of the chapter (25) by saying, *"I thank God – through Jesus Christ our Lord!"*

Romans 8:1 says, *"There is therefore now no condemnation to them which are in Christ Jesus, who walk not after the flesh, but after the spirit."* In other words, it is inevitable that we are going to sin, we are going to mess up and we are going to fall short of the high standard of God's law. But when this happens and when we fall down, we don't have to stay down. Satan would love to keep us down, but the devil is a liar! You can get back up again and ask the Lord to forgive you, trusting Him to do the rest.

Today, there are many people who are frustrated over their inability to stay on the right path. We struggle daily to fight off our temptations, but the mere fact that it bothers you means you are no longer at war with God. Like Paul, we accept God's moral standards. That's precisely the reason why we become angry and frustrated with ourselves when we miss the mark. Through God's law, we are presented with a high standard by which we are to live and govern ourselves. Thus, when each one of us stands before the law, we will fall short every time.

The "law" in the Old Testament was a set of standards that had to be followed, or else! But Romans 6:14 tells us, *"For sin shall not have dominion over you: for ye are not under the law, but under Grace."* In other words, we now look to the gospel of Jesus Christ to show us the standard which we should live by. Our motivation to measure up now comes from the fact that when we fail, the grace of Jesus Christ will make up the difference every time!

Over and over again, as we miss the mark and sin, we will become frustrated with our actions. But when we say, "Oops…" that's really a manifestation of the Holy Spirit convicting us and working on us to bring us back into accountability. Hebrews 12:6-8 says, *"For whom the Lord loves He chastens, and scourges every son whom He receives. If you endure chastening, God deals with you as with sons; for what son is there whom a father does not chasten? But if you are without chastening, of which all have become partakers, then you are illegitimate and not sons."*

As believers, we should be grateful that the work of the gospel is there for us every time we say, "Oops, I did it again!" It whips us until we correct our actions. As a young boy, oft times my father would discipline me with corporal punishment (a nice way of saying whippings) but I now realize that can't nobody whip you like the Lord can!

Finally, my brothers and sisters let me leave you with this. When we're talking about the "carnal" man within us, "Oops, I did it again!" refers to an instance in which we did something we did NOT want to do. But when we're talking about our gratitude towards God, those same words can take on a completely different meaning! Paul says God's saving grace excites him so much that he must give Him thanks!

This reminds me of the old lady who moved in with her grandchildren up North. Her grandchildren were wealthy professionals who attended this "quiet" church in the big city. Every Sunday morning before church, they had to give

Grandmother a reminder course in church etiquette. They asked Grandmother to keep in mind that she wasn't down South anymore and informed her that the dignified people in their church don't shout "Amen" or "Hallelujah" like she was accustomed to back home at her church. They pleaded with Grandmother not to embarrass them.

Every Sunday, Grandmother tried her best to keep quiet during church. Her grandchildren would notice when the Spirit started moving through Grandmother, and they would give her the eye so she would hold her peace. They didn't mind the funny-looking red coat Grandmother wore. They didn't mind the flower that dangled from her church hat. If only she could sit there quietly, they'd be happy.

Well, one Sunday morning, a guest preacher from down South was invited to grace the pulpit. During his sermon, the preacher started talking about the goodness of Jesus. He began to talk about how God can make a way out of no way. He talked about how God had protected him down through the years from dangers seen and unseen. He talked about how God is a way maker! He talked about how God is the doctor who made the doctor! Grandmother started patting her feet.

He talked about how God so loved the world that He gave His only begotten Son, Jesus Christ! He told them how Jesus gave His life by dying on an old, rugged cross! Grandmother started waving her hands in the air. The kids gave her the eye, but Grandmother couldn't hold her peace! That country preacher continued to share how they took Him down from the cross and placed Him in a borrowed tomb. He told them how the Lord remained in the grave for three days and three nights, but early Sunday morning, He arose with all power in His hands!

Grandmother tried her best to contain her excitement as her grandchildren had requested, but when she began to think about what the Lord had done for her, she just couldn't hold her peace. She started shouting and praising God all over that church! Finally, after she had finished shouting, she opened her eyes to see her grandchildren (along with the rest of the snooty congregation) staring at her. The only thing Grandmother could say was, "Oops, I did it again!"

I don't know about you, but I can relate to that grandmother. Because when I think of the goodness of Jesus and all He's done for me, it doesn't matter where I am or who's watching me: I just can't hold my peace! I said I wasn't gone tell nobody...but, "Oops, I did it again!"

Disclaimer: For more than twenty years since my ordination, I have been privileged to share with God's people many, many sermons and Bible studies. Often, preachers absorb others' words and insights without knowing or remembering their original source. If any of the above seems somehow familiar, please accept my humble apologies. I have not wittingly reproduced any writing as my own that should be otherwise acknowledged.

Reflections

_____

_____

_____

_____

_____

_____

_____

_____

_____

_____

_____

_____

_____

_____

_____

_____

Chapter 1
Just Forget About It

Many of you find it difficult to move forward because you can't seem to let go of your past. You're left with feelings of guilt and shame as your past sins keep resurfacing: suicide attempts, abortions, felony convictions, infidelity and a host of other mistakes. Sometimes, the decisions we make in life create a wedge between us and God, causing us to run away from Him. However, God never leaves us. Jesus, in turn, extends His nailed scared hands, making it clear to him: that whatever he's done was nailed to the cross, and he's welcomed back in the arms of Jesus.

You may remember the parable of the Prodigal Son (Luke 15:11-32). Here, the younger of two sons disrespects his father by prematurely demanding his inheritance. The son goes on to denounce his religion and his God. He takes his inheritance and flees to a distant land, where he wastes his fortune on wild living.

Naturally, he runs out of money. When a severe famine hits the country, the son finds himself in dire circumstances. He is forced to take a job feeding pigs and is so destitute that he longs to eat the food given to the pigs. The young man finally comes to his senses and remembers his father. With humility, he recognizes his foolishness and decides to return to his father and ask for forgiveness and mercy. His father, who had been watching and waiting, receives his son back with open arms.

The parable of the Prodigal Son is a beautiful reflection of the grace and forgiveness of our Heavenly Father. Typically, a son received his inheritance at the time of his father's death. For the younger brother to instigate the early division of the family estate showed a rebellious and proud disregard for his father's authority, not to mention a selfish and immature attitude. Yet his father received him back after all he had done.

This story is an extreme case of blatant disrespect for which the son should have been cut off from his father. In the same way, how many times have we displayed momentary lapses in judgment and totally disrespected our Heavenly Father? If we're honest, we'd all have to admit that we've had moments in our lives when we've been in the pigs' pen. And because of our past actions, we run away from God, and we believe it's impossible to come back after sinking so low. The truth, though, is that it doesn't matter what you've done. We serve a God who says, "I'm waiting for you with open arms. Come back home!"

Back in the 1980s, I was a teenager. Raised in church, I was trying my best to live for God while struggling with the actions and behaviors typical of most teenagers. Around 1985, I became a huge fan of a contemporary gospel group called Commissioned. In particular, their song "Running

Back To You" spoke directly to my heart and changed my life forever.

The lyrics include a detailed conversation between a down and out believer and the Lord. At his lowest point he is convinced, that because of his indiscretions and wicked ways, he has reached a point of no return. Pursuing his own desires on worldly things, he literally turns his back on God. At one point in the song, he even tries to tell the Lord that He doesn't understand. Jesus in turn, extends His nailed scared hands, making it clear to this person: that he's welcomed back in the arms of Jesus.

I encourage you to pause and meditate on the lyrics of this powerful song, which still ministers to the hearts of so many struggling Christians today. I even encourage you to watch the YouTube video of Commissioned performing it live during their reunion tour in 2009: http://youtu.be/QtOOOq5NWnU. As well, this song will help you understand how the grace of God is far greater than your sins. Even though you have committed great sins, you need to realize that the blood of Jesus Christ is still greater.

If you are new to Christianity and find this concept hard to comprehend, don't feel bad. It still blows my mind today! But the reality is that God can, and does, forgive us at our worst. So if He forgives and forgets our indiscretions, why can't we? It is clear throughout the Bible that God not only forgives our sins, but He forgets them as well. Take a moment to read and meditate on the following scriptures:

> Hebrew 8:12, *"For I will be merciful to their unrighteousness, and their sins and their lawless deeds I will remember no more."*

Jeremiah 31:34, *"…For I will forgive their iniquity, and their sin I will remember no more."*

Isaiah 43:25, *"I, even I, am He who blots out your transgressions for My own sake; and I will not remember your sins."*

As you have just read, when we seek God's forgiveness with our heart, His forgiveness is immediate and complete. Our almighty, all-powerful and all-knowing God loves us so much that He doesn't hold our forgiven transgressions against us. Why? Because the blood of His Son Jesus Christ washes them away!

As believers, we can rest in this truth and rejoice in the certainty that the Lord will not remember our sins anymore. Why should we? 1 John 1:9 tells us, *"If we confess our sins, He is faithful and just and will forgive us our sins and purify us from all unrighteousness."*

In the Bible, the word "condemnation" simply means to fall short of God's glory. Many of God's people are living under a heavy burden of guilt and shame because of their past. As a result, they find it difficult to believe that God will forgive and forget their sins. The act of condemning (or condemnation) will bring unrelenting feelings of guilt and shame, with no hope of mercy or freedom, but the devil is a liar! Romans 8:1-2 says, *"There is therefore now no condemnation to those who are in Christ Jesus, who do not walk according to the flesh, but according to the Spirit. For the law of the Spirit of life in Christ Jesus has made me free from the law of sin and death."*

So what's the next step after you've asked for forgiveness? How do you become liberated from your feelings of guilt and shame? Paul gives us the answer in Philippians 3:12-14, *"Not that I have already attained, or am already perfected; but I press on, that I may lay hold of that for which Christ Jesus has also laid hold of me; Brethren, I do not count myself to have apprehended; but one thing I do, forgetting those things which are behind and reaching forward to those things which are ahead, I press toward the goal for the prize of the upward call of God in Christ Jesus."*

I remember visiting with my former pastor during a rough patch in my life. I sat in his study and proceeded to beat myself up over a collection of past mistakes that I had made. As always, my pastor injected a healthy dose of motivational nuggets into my sprit, but the words of wisdom that lifted my spirit were "Your past is not fatal, your mistakes are not final, and your failure is not the end." This statement spoke volumes to me, so much so that I have passed it on to countless others who have a hard time letting go of their past.

You will never become the man or woman that God has called you to be if you allow yourself to be held hostage by the guilt and shame of your past mistakes. It doesn't matter who you are; every last one of us will make mistakes in life. Throughout our lives, we are constantly learning; thus, true wisdom and spiritual maturity are exercised only when we learn from our past mistakes.

Satan would love to keep you in chains from the bondages of your sin, but you don't have to be a slave to your past indiscretions. You are free through the precious blood of Jesus Christ! John 8:34-36 says, *Jesus answered them, "Most assuredly, I say to you, whoever commits sin is a slave of sin. And a slave does not abide in the house forever, but a son abides forever. Therefore if the Son makes you free, you shall be free indeed."*

Sure, you've made some mistakes along the way, and you're going to make many more during the course of your life! You might have even veered off course, but your spiritual navigational guide keeps saying, "Recalculating!" In other words, you might have fallen down, but you don't have to stay there. You can get back up again in the Name of Jesus Christ!

As believers, we can rejoice in the fact that God doesn't erase our future because of our past! I encourage you to forget about what happened in your past and move forward with the following declaration:

I will pursue what I know is His call on my life, regardless of my past mistakes and indiscretions. I will not allow the enemy to convince me that I am unqualified to become what God has called me to be because of my struggles with sin. No longer will I be bound by the shackles of sin and shame. I will move forward with the power of the Holy Spirit, rise above my past mistakes, and believe with every fiber of my being that "greater is He that is in me than he who is in the world!" I accept the fact that I am not perfect, but God still loves me unconditionally. I will forgive myself and leave the past behind me. Most importantly, I will receive the forgiveness of God and press forward toward the ultimate goal: the prize of the upward call of God in Christ Jesus!

Reflections

_____

_____

_____

_____

_____

_____

_____

_____

_____

_____

_____

_____

_____

_____

_____

_____

_____

Chapter 2
Stop Faking It

It has become common in many American churches for Christians to pretend that everything is fine and dandy in our lives, even though we know that's the furthest thing from the truth. Furthermore, throughout Christian history, misconceptions about what characteristics define a true Christian have formed. Many people believe that good Christians should always have a smile on their face and a bubbly, pleasant personality. If by chance they're confronted by a challenging circumstance or experience, they should put up a façade and pretend as if everything is just fine.

Unfortunately, an unwritten rule seems to exist in many Christian churches and religious circles these days: Everybody seems to be faking it. We go to great lengths trying to fool people into believing that we're more spiritual than we really are. We put up a front so that people will think that we believe God is in control of our situation when in reality, that's not at all what we believe.

We pretend that our faith gauge is on full when we're actually running on fumes. We do a great job of concealing the imperfections in various parts of our lives, because we've learned how to fake people out. We pretend that we have the perfect marriage when we're living in separate bedrooms and barely speaking to our spouse. We pretend that our children are perfect. We pretend that we aren't living from paycheck to paycheck. We pretend that we're not being overtaken by this pressure cooker we call life.

Some people will go so far as to practice their Christian walk in the mirror, so they're able to strut in the church on Sunday mornings and fool all the other saints with their customary greeting, "Child...God is good all the time, and all the time God is good!" We have become experts at pretending. We pretend that we've got it all together, so much so that we could never be forthcoming about our sin to others!

It has become second nature for most Christians to play make believe. We give quick and efficient responses when someone probes into our lives. If someone asks how we're doing, we paint that superficial smile across our faces and respond by saying, "Oh, I'm better than blessed!" This answer is much easier than saying, "Honestly, I feel like all hell has broken loose in my life!" Imagine the look on the person's face if you said, "I got fired from my job, my wife/husband doesn't love me, my kids have lost their minds, and my dog won't even greet me when I come home!" One thing is for certain; you wouldn't have to worry about them asking you about your personal life ever again!

In his book *Messy Spirituality*, Mike Yaconell eloquently writes: *"Pretending is the grease of modern non-relationships. When we fake it or pretend that all is well, it perpetuates the illusion of relationships, by connecting us on the basis of who we aren't!."*

By no means should this suggest that you have to share all of your problems with the world, but Yaconell's point is that all of this pretending is sending many people into a downward spiral of depression. Why? Because of all these false appearances, many people start to feel like no one can possibly relate to their situation. They become convinced that everyone seems to have it all together, except for them!

However, the reality is that most people really aren't who they appear to be. We all have our secrets, our skeletons and individual issues, because we all sin. It doesn't matter who you are or how long you've been saved; everyone struggles with sin and must ask the Lord for forgiveness on a continual basis.

The biggest misconception of Christians is that we don't sin, but this is certainly not the case. The Bible is clear when we read 1 John 1:8, *"If we say that we have no sin, we deceive ourselves and the truth is not in us."* As well, Romans 3:10, *"… there is none righteous, no, not one;"* In other words, everyone struggles with sin from time to time. True liberation comes only when we refuse to pretend, fake, lie or allow others to believe that we are something or someone that we're not! I think we forget that God has His eyes on us at all times, lending truth to that 80s hit song "I Always Feel Like Somebody's Watching Me!"

David was able to deceive the people of Israel about his sins with Bathsheba and the assassination of her husband Uriah that he ordered, but he couldn't fool God! God saw everything, and David confirms this in Psalms 139:2-3.

He says, *"You know my sitting down and my rising up; You understand my thought afar off. You comprehend my path and my lying down, and are acquainted with all my ways."*

Even more, Jesus says in Luke 12:2, *"For there is nothing covered that will not be revealed, nor hidden that will not be known."* In other words, what's done in the dark will ultimately come to the light! However, the all-seeing eyes of God should encourage us, because it's comforting to know that we serve a God who sees us in our weaknesses and still decides to love us.

Stop faking it! You're not fooling anyone but yourself! God hates sin, but He doesn't hate the man or the woman who commits the sin. He loves us unconditionally! Dottie Rambo says it best in her song "He Looked Beyond My Faults." God sees everything we do and knows our true selves, including our strengths and weaknesses. We might be able to hide our weaknesses and conceal our sins from friends and family, but when we cheat, steal, lie or misrepresent ourselves, God sees it all. We might be successful at fooling others, but we can't fool God. God is watching us at all times, not to spy on us, but to protect us, provide for us and guide us while we're on this tedious journey. I don't know about you, but I'm thankful and relieved to know God is watching over me.

As I encourage you to stop faking it, let me reiterate that God forgives us when we repent. Through the precious blood of our Lord and Savior Jesus Christ, He gives us another chance! God doesn't see what we are today but, rather, our potential! Sometimes we can only see our weakness, but God sees our strength! When we have failed miserably and sadness clouds our vision, sometimes the only thing we can see is defeat, but God sees our ultimate victory!

It's easy for people to accept the notion that only those outside the Christian community have problems with sin. However, this book is targeted to those within the faith who find themselves struggling with sin. More than ever before, believers are abandoning the church and some have given up on their faith altogether because of their ongoing struggle with sin. The reality, however, is this: From the front door to the pulpit, every last one of us has to deal with sin and the consequences when we get off track.

The self-proclaimed super Christian will have a problem with me saying this, because it goes against everything we've been taught since Sunday school. But I have a real passion for the under-achiever Christian, the silent majority who repeatedly says, "I'm never going to get this Christianity thing right!" A Gospel message of hope and encouragement needs to be spoken continuously to those struggling in their faith because of their inability to avoid sin. The truth is that there is no such thing as a Christian who doesn't sin!

Throughout the Bible, we discover that many of our heroes were flawed individuals: Eve ate the fruit, Cain killed Abel, Noah got drunk, Moses murdered a man, Samson liked his women, David had an affair and ordered the assassination of his lover's husband, Solomon got a big head, Jonah refused to obey, Peter denied the Lord, Thomas doubted, and Paul persecuted Christians. These are just a few examples of the men and women throughout the Bible who sinned, but God loved them in spite of it.

The Greek word most commonly translated as "sin" simply means "to miss the mark." In modern usage, the word "sin" means to commit an error or an act that violates God's will. When we fall short of the standards set by God, or when we miss the mark, we sin. All people sin, because we are all made of flesh, and our nature is to do the things of the flesh. However, we are all called to obey God, so God made a provision to forgive all who come into obedience.

Hebrews 5:9 says, *"And being made perfect, He became the author of eternal salvation unto all them that obey him;"* These people will not be punished for their sins, but instead, they shall be forgiven. This is eternal salvation, or what we believers call "being saved" or "being born again."

Sin is a universal problem for all mankind; it's something that every human being does. Many of you have said, "I hate sinning! I feel terrible afterwards when I do something I know I'm not supposed to do. Why can't I live a life free of sin?" The Apostle Paul expressed the same frustration with sin that we deal with today. Read what he wrote in Romans 7:14-25:

"So the trouble is not with the law, for it is spiritual and good. The trouble is with me, for I am all too human, a slave to sin. I don't really understand myself, for I want to do what is right, but I don't do it. Instead, I do what I hate. But if I know that what I am doing is wrong, this shows that I agree that the law is good. So I am not the one doing wrong; it is sin living in me that does it. And I know that nothing good lives in me, that is, in my sinful nature. I want to do what is right, but I can't. I want to do what is good, but I don't. I don't want to do what is wrong, but I do it anyway."

"But if I do what I don't want to do, I am not really the one doing wrong; it is sin living in me that does it. I have discovered this principle of life—that when I want to do what is right, I inevitably do what is wrong. I love God's law with all my heart.

But there is another power within me that is at war with my mind. This power makes me a slave to the sin that is still within me. Oh, what a miserable person I am! Who will free me from this life that is dominated by sin and death? Thank God! The answer is in Jesus Christ our Lord. So you see how it is: In my mind I really want to obey God's law, but because of my sinful nature I am a slave to sin."

Even though we don't want to sin, the reality is that we must ask God for forgiveness on a continual basis, because it is inevitable that we will sin! Paul said in Romans 7:16-18 that as a physical being, *"Sin dwells in me. For I know that in me (that is, in my flesh) nothing good dwells; for to will is present with me, but how to perform what is good I do not find."* Our natural ability to live up to righteous standards and values is limited. Although we strive to do our best not to sin, we will repeatedly miss the mark and fall short of the conduct that God expects of us.

Paul explains why we sin and why we miss the mark on a continual basis: As creatures of the flesh, it is in our nature to sin. Even Jesus identifies the most significant cause of sin as the flesh. He said in Matthew 26:41, *"Watch and pray, lest you enter into temptation. The spirit indeed is willing, but the flesh is weak."* Simply put, it is the weakness of the flesh that gives birth to sin!

Like Paul, Jesus explained that although we desire to do what is right, we will often fail because our resolve is weak. In other words, our flesh is vulnerable to temptation. I think of George Clinton's hit song entitled "Atomic Dog." The dog asks the question, "Why must I feel like that? Why must I chase the cat?" Then he answers himself, "It's nothin' but the dog in me!"

In essence, the Atomic Dog was saying that his actions and behavior were the result of his DNA, and his doggish nature would surface whether he liked it or not! Now, I am in no way suggesting that anyone reading this book is a dog! I do, however, make this comparison, because many of us are left feeling frustrated at our inability to avoid sin. As long as we posses these earthly (carnal) bodies, we will constantly have a struggle with sin. Why? Because of our doggish (sinful) nature!

Furthermore, our physical bodies subject us to weaknesses that can lead to sin. Understand that our flesh is not evil; rather, it is inherently weak. Therefore, our appetites tempt us to sin. James 1:14-15 makes it clear that sin arises through our human desires: *"Each one is tempted when he is drawn away by his own desires and enticed. Then, when desire has conceived, it gives birth to sin…"*

Even with our most earnest attempts, we cannot keep ourselves from sin. God is the only One who can keep us from sin. We might desire to do good, but if we don't turn to Jesus and let Him work through us, we will fail regardless of how much we hate sin. Hebrews 9:22 gives us the costly price of God's forgiveness: *"Without the shedding of Blood, there is no forgiveness."* In the Old Testament, the continual sacrifices of unblemished lambs were required to satisfy God's wrath and judgment for sins. But John 3:16 tells us, *"For God so loved the world that He gave His only begotten Son, that whoever believes in Him will not perish but have everlasting life."*

Jesus died on a Roman cross and literally became the ultimate sacrifice for our sins. Romans 6:23 says, *"For the wages of sin is death, but the gift of God is eternal life in Christ Jesus our Lord."*

Our sin debt had to be paid, and the only acceptable form of payment was the precious blood of Jesus Christ. 1 John 1:7 says, *"But if we walk in the light as He is in the light, we have fellowship with one another, and the blood of Jesus Christ His Son cleanses us from all sin."*

What a wonderful Savior! Jesus paid a debt that He did not owe, because we owed a debt that we could not pay! Colossians 2:13-14 says, *"And you, being dead in your trespasses and the uncircumcision of your flesh, He has made alive together with Him, having forgiven you all trespasses, having wiped out the handwriting of requirements that was against us, which was contrary to us. And He has taken it out of the way, having nailed it to the cross."*

Again, let me repeat that we don't have the green light to go out and sin whenever we feel the urge. Just because you are saved does not by any means entitle you to do whatever it is that you'd like to do. You *do not* have a license to sin! However, it is important that you understand that even though you will sin, mess up and miss the mark on a continual basis, God still loves you unconditionally!

We as believers are the recipients of His Grace and Mercy, both of which will be explained in the next chapter. If you are a Christian, you will sin! But 1 John 1:9 encourages us by saying, *"If we confess our sins, he is faithful and just to forgive us our sins, and to cleanse us from all unrighteousness."* God will forgive you of any sin if you are a believer; the blood of Jesus has already washed your sins away.

As we close this chapter, I encourage you to take a few moments to talk with God. Ask Him to forgive you of your trespasses and restore you to the place where you can be all that He has called you to be. If you need help starting your prayer, I would suggest you begin with David's prayer in Psalms 51:1-4 & 7-12. David prayed these words after he had sinned but desired to be reconciled with God:

"Have mercy upon me, O God, according to Your loving-kindness; according to the multitude of Your tender mercies, blot out my transgressions. Wash me thoroughly from my iniquity, and cleanse me from my sin. For I acknowledge my transgressions, and my sin is always before me. Against You, You only, have I sinned, and done this evil in Your sight, that You may be found just when You speak, and blameless when You judge. Purge me with hyssop, and I shall be clean; Wash me, and I shall be whiter than snow. Make me hear joy and gladness, that the bones You have broken may rejoice. Hide Your face from my sins, and blot out all my iniquities. Create in me a clean heart, O God, and renew a steadfast spirit within me. Do not cast me away from Your presence, and do not take Your Holy Spirit from me. Restore to me the joy of Your salvation, and uphold me by Your generous Spirit."

Reflections

_____

_____

_____

_____

_____

_____

_____

_____

_____

_____

_____

_____

_____

_____

_____

_____

_____

Chapter 3
His Grace and Mercy

Many people sit in the church every Sunday and listen to their pastor talk about God's Grace and Mercy. However, most of them couldn't articulate or explain the difference between the two, because they really don't fully understand it themselves. Let's use this chapter to get a full understanding of what Grace and Mercy are all about.

Consider Grace and Mercy as inseparable twins. Grace and Mercy usually travel together. If by chance one is encountered alone, the other will not be far away. Grace is defined by Webster's Dictionary as: "1) beneficence or generosity shown by God to man, especially divine favor unmerited by man: the mercy of God as distinguished from his justice; 2) a short prayer either asking a blessing before or giving thanks after a meal; 3) a disposition to kindness, favor, clemency or compassion: benign goodwill; the display of kindly treatment usually on the part of a superior."

Mercy, is defined by Webster's as: "1) compassion or forbearance shown to an offender or subject; clemency or kindness extended to someone instead of strictness or severity; 2) a blessing regarded as an act of divine favor or compassion; 3) relief of distress; compassion shown to victims of misfortune."

As you have just read, the English language definitions of these words are quite similar. Therefore, I believe the simplest and shortest way to define Grace and Mercy is to say:

> Grace: Is when God *DOES* give us what we *DON'T* deserve!
> Mercy: Is when God *DOESN'T* give us what we *DO* deserve!

Grace is a gift from God the Father. It is not earned as an action one expects payment for. It is not an obligation imposed on God for something we have done. His Grace is a gift. A gift is something that is extended freely (or voluntarily) from the giver to the recipient. John 3:16, *"For God so loved the world that He **gave** His only begotten son…"* Furthermore, God told Paul in 2 Corinthians 12:9, *"My grace is sufficient for thee: for my strength is made perfect in weakness."*

Grace could also be defined as God's sufficiency or God's fullness in the life of the believer. In essence, when we accept Jesus Christ as our personal Lord and Savior, we have stood before the throne of God who, in His Mercy, was gracious enough to provide a way to gain access to Him. However, this access was closed due to the sin of Adam and Eve, and if not for the Grace of God, would have been permanently closed.

Throughout His Word, God reveals the proper standards for our behavior. As we discussed in the last chapter, when we miss the mark or fall short of those standards, we sin. His Word makes us painfully aware of our shortcomings and also informs us when we are not pleasing God. It points out to us our need for the saving Grace of God, which is provided for us by His mercy through His Son, Jesus Christ.

Grace is God's unmerited favor shown toward us. At its core, that's what Christianity is all about: the Amazing Grace of God! Arguably, God's Grace is what draws people to Christianity. Islam has a strict code of law that all Muslims must follow. Those who belong to the Jewish faith must obey the covenant in order to receive God's blessings. Hindus believe in the doctrine of karma. Buddhists follow an eightfold path to righteousness. In one way or another, every religion of the world requires people to earn God's approval. Every religion except Christianity. The concepts of Grace and God's unconditional love are completely unique to the Christian faith.

The Bible mentions Grace 170 times. Grace is sometimes manifested through God's actions. God does many good things for us which we don't deserve. Grace is also shown through God's blessings. We receive undeserved eternal life and the promise of heaven. Once you understand the concept of Grace, you'll see how it's necessary for our salvation.

Ephesians 2:8 says, *"For by grace are ye saved through faith; and that not of yourselves: it is the gift of God..."* We don't earn salvation. We don't deserve salvation. The crucial aspect of salvation is the term "justification." To be justified means to declare or make righteous in the sight of God. Justification is God's declaration of those who receive Christ as righteous, because Christ's righteousness is imputed to those who receive Him. 2 Corinthians 5:21 says, *"For He made Him who knew no sin to be sin for us, that we might become the righteousness of God in Him."*

The Bible makes it crystal clear that we are justified by the Grace of God. For example, Romans 3:24 says, *"Being justified freely by his grace through the redemption that is in Christ Jesus:"* Titus 3:7 goes on to say, *"That being justified by his grace, we should be made heirs according to the hope of eternal life."* Therefore, justification is the act by which we are saved by God on the basis of the payment that Jesus Christ made for our sins on a hill called Calvary.

Not only are we saved by the Grace of God, but we also serve the Lord and live the Christian life by the Grace of God. The letters of Paul repeatedly speak of a blessing of Grace, along with peace, for believers. Paul writes in Romans 1:6-7, *"among whom you also are the called of Jesus Christ; To all who are in Rome, beloved of God, called to be saints: Grace to you and peace from God our Father and the Lord Jesus Christ."* Who is Paul speaking to here? He's speaking to the believers who are already saved and on their way to heaven. As evidenced by this text, he recognizes that they also need Grace for living the Christian life!

In 1 Corinthians 15:10, Paul explains the Grace by which we live: *"But by the Grace of God I am what I am: and his grace which was bestowed upon me was not in vain; but I labored more abundantly than they all: yet not I, but the grace of God which was with me."* From this verse, we see that it was God's Grace that made Paul who he was! It was God's goodness working in Paul that made him such a great servant of God.

Obviously, we need the Grace of God as well. We need it first of all for our salvation, because without the Grace of God, we cannot have eternal life. But we also need the Grace of God for our daily walk with Him. Jesus tells us in John 15:5, *"I am the vine, you are the branches. He who abides in Me, and I in him, bears much fruit; for without Me you can do nothing."* In other words, we can do nothing without Him.

God provides us with daily strength through His Grace. We should believe that He will provide what He has promised and walk with a newfound confidence, knowing that His Grace is working in us! The concept of God's Grace and Mercy is an integral part of the gospel message, because His compassion toward us is the foundation upon which our salvation is based.

On the other hand, Mercy is shown through God's withholding of the judgment which we do deserve. We have sinned against God and continue to violate His laws. According to Romans 6:23, we have earned the "wages of sin" which is death, and we are condemned already if we do not believe in the name of Jesus Christ as our Savior. Technically, God has every right to judge us, find us guilty and sentence us to the lake of fire.

Because of God's Mercy we as believers do not receive the judgment of God against our sins! The prophet Daniel declares in Daniel 9:9, *"To the Lord our God belong mercy and forgiveness, though we have rebelled against Him."*

We deserve judgment, but Mercy prevails, and God withholds the punishment called for by our sin. Jeremiah expresses the same idea in Lamentations 3:22-23: *"Through the LORD's mercies we are not consumed, because His compassions fail not. They are new every morning; great is Your faithfulness."*

Understanding the true depth of God's Mercy means understanding the depth of our own neediness. We have no hope except through God's merciful activity on our behalf.

We must recognize that we come before God bringing nothing but our own sinfulness, just as the publican in the parable (Luke 13:18) brought nothing when he prayed, *"God be merciful to me a sinner."*

Because of Mercy, God withholds His judgment for our sins, but Mercy delivers you only if you receive Christ as your Savior. You must believe that He died not only for your sins, but that He died in your place in order to pay your penalty. In your own time, look up the following scriptures relating to Grace and Mercy.

God's Grace

+ Grace is shown by God: Ezra 9:8
+ Grace is given by God: Psalms 84:11
+ Grace is obtained by a sinner: Proverbs 3:34
+ Grace is a gift from God: Romans 5:15
+ Grace helps us grow and gain knowledge: John 1:17
+ Grace justifies us: Romans 3:24
+ We are saved by Grace: Ephesians 2:5, Ephesians 2:8

God's Mercy

+ Mercy guides the people of God: Exodus 15:13
+ Mercy is given to those who love God: Exodus 20:6
+ Mercy forgives: Numbers 14:18-19
+ Mercy endures forever: Psalms 9:13
+ Mercy is God's response to our afflictions: Psalms 25:16

+ Mercy is God's response to our cries for help: Psalms 27:7
+ Mercy is God's response to our enemies: Psalms 136:24, Psalms 143:12

Reflections

_____

_____

_____

_____

_____

_____

_____

_____

_____

_____

_____

_____

_____

_____

_____

_____

Chapter 4
A God of a ~~Second~~ Another Chance

More often than we might suspect, many believers end up in a familiar place during their walk with Christ. Initially, we start out with the very best of intentions. We are excited and on fire with a strong passion to succeed in the faith. We have a strong desire to be faithful followers of Jesus Christ and save the world. Yet, very often, we become distracted along the way and allow sin and the wrong influences to enter our lives. A few bad decisions are made, and we might even experience a moral challenge or a setback which causes our relationship with Christ to suffer.

In the 11th chapter of 2 Samuel, David commits a whole series of sins connected to his adulterous relationship with Bathsheba. Lust leads to adultery, adultery leads to deception, and deception leads to murder. Many people read the story of David and Bathsheba as a story of judgment and condemnation. But if you have experienced divorce, moral failures and random lapses in judgment, you might be inclined to view this story as I do: as a story of God's Grace, forgiveness and restoration for ordinary people who are called to do extraordinary work!

My prayer is that you'll be encouraged after revisiting this familiar story, realizing that God loves you unconditionally and desires to forgive you and restore your relationship with Him. I don't want to assume that everyone is familiar with the story of David and Bathsheba, so I'll provide you with a brief overview.

Basically, this is a story about King David, a man of God, who messed up in a major way. David's behavior was not what you would expect from a good, God-fearing man. The sins David committed were not accidental indiscretions, but rather continual premeditated lapses in judgment. David put a great deal of thought and effort into committing his sin and went to even greater lengths to cover it up. When it was all said and done, two families were destroyed, and two people died.

However, an amazing fact about this story provides us with encouragement: David wasn't ruined by this situation. Not only was he able to recover from the mistakes he had made, but he went on to become the man who God had called him to be. The same man who had an affair and committed murder is also the one known as "A MAN AFTER GOD'S OWN HEART!" But I digress…

Here's a quick overview of the story. One night, a restless King David went out on the balcony of his palace to get some fresh air. To his amazement, across the way, he saw this beautiful woman, Bathsheba, taking a bath. Through an inquiry, David discovered that her husband, Uriah, was a soldier away at war, so David made his move! He sent for Bathsheba and seduced her. She became pregnant, precipitating David's attempt to cover up his tracks. David called for Uriah to come in from the battlefield for a time of rest and relaxation with his wife.

Uriah politely refused David's thoughtfulness, because going home to his wife during a time of war would have been disloyal to his fellow soldiers. Since Uriah couldn't be persuaded, David sent him back to battle with a letter to deliver to the commanding officer. Uriah didn't realize it, but he was delivering his own death warrant. The letter instructed the commanding officer to not only place Uriah on the front line of battle, but also to withdraw the other troops as well. Sure enough, Uriah was killed, and David subsequently married Bathsheba.

The Lord was incredibly displeased with what David had done. David knew that he had done wrong and that he couldn't get away with it any longer. God sent a prophet named Nathan to confront David about his sin. David and Bathsheba's newborn child was very sick, and Nathan made it clear that it was all David's fault because of his sin. David felt horrible. He had gotten so far off track that he had to make things right with God. This is the time at which he wrote the 51st Psalm.

When you have a moment, I encourage you to read the entire 51st Psalm. It provides a road map to redemption for those who have gotten off track, but has a desire for reconciliation with a God who cares. We learn from David's story that no matter how badly we mess up, we can always return to God. You might have committed what society views as a big sin, but the degrees of sin are judged only in the eyes of society.

There are no big and little sins in God's eyes. When we sin, God wants to forgive us and help us to get back on the right track, but we have to make some changes on our part.

Notice how David begins Psalms 51:1-2: *"Have mercy upon me, O God, According to Your loving-kindness; according to the multitude of Your tender mercies, Blot out my transgressions. Wash me thoroughly from my iniquity, And cleanse me from my sin."*

We often deny or try to justify our sins for as long as we think we can get away with it. David knew he was guilty and could no longer deny his wrongdoings. He longed for the day where the dark cloud that followed him would be removed. And so, from the depths of his heart, David repented and asked God for forgiveness.

We often approach our own sin this way. We deny, justify or pretend that our situation isn't so bad. We might even be able to tell others that what we're doing isn't really sin, but as long as we maintain this defiant attitude, it is impossible for us to get right with God. If we truly desire to reconcile and get right with God, we must have a change of heart.

When I got in trouble as a child, my father always asked me if I was sorry for what I had done. Of course, my answer was always yes! But my father continued his questioning by asking if I was sorry for what I did or if I was just sorry that I had gotten caught. Remorse is an emotional expression of personal regret, a lesson my father taught me at an early age. A change of heart, however, means that we are truly sorry for our actions, regardless of who knows or doesn't know about our indiscretion.

Most of us are quick to accept or take credit for our accomplishments. However, when it comes to our failures, we're quick to point the finger or place the blame on someone else. Shifting the blame can be traced all the way back to the Garden of Eden. When God frowned on Adam for eating the forbidden fruit, Adam didn't admit that it was his fault for disobeying God. Instead, he said, "It was that woman You gave me. It's all her fault!" Adam threw Eve under the bus! Eve, in turn, passed the blame onto the serpent.

President Harry S. Truman was famous for a small sign he placed on his desk. The sign simply read, "The buck stops here." It meant he wouldn't pass the blame or throw anyone under the bus for his actions or inaction. Truman made it clear that he would take responsibility for anything good or bad that happened during his administration. Sometimes, it can be very difficult, uncomfortable and embarrassing to accept responsibility for our actions, but if we truly desire to get our lives back on track, we must accept responsibility for our actions.

David could have very easily said, "Bathsheba should have put up a shower curtain. I had no choice but to look at her!" He could have blamed his infidelity on any one of his wives (he had at least eight) for not meeting his needs. The blame game could have gone on and on, but instead, David decided to take ownership of his actions. As he sings in Psalms 51:4, *"Against You, You only, have I sinned, And done this evil in Your sight – That You may be found just when You speak, And blameless when You judge."*

In essence, David was saying, "The buck stops here! No one else is to blame for my actions." We continue to find ourselves in our uncompromising situations, because we take our eyes off God, making it easy to become distracted. David's life got off track, because he decided to chart his own path and do things his way. Through several failed attempts to cover up his mess, David realized that things had gotten out of control. In order for him to make things right with God, he had to have a change of mind.

Read his words from Psalms 51:7-11: *"Purge me with hyssop, and I shall be clean; Wash me, and I shall be whiter than snow. Make me hear joy and gladness, that the bones You have broken may rejoice. Hide Your face from my sins, And blot out all my iniquities. Create in me a clean heart, O God, And renew a steadfast spirit within me. Do not cast me away from Your presence, And do not take Your Holy Spirit from me."*

Whenever we try to fix our own mess, we usually end up with a bigger mess than when we started. If you've gotten off track because of a mess you've made, you're going to need the Lord to get you back on the right track. There is no problem, circumstance or situation too hard for God to fix. Many people will never find their way back to God, because they believe they must clean up what they've messed up. But God will take you just as you are! He wants to forgive you, cleanse you and wash you white as snow.

When you sin, you need to repent. Naturally, there will be feelings of guilt, but if you feel guilty too long, then you haven't really repented. Repentance results in joy. Repentance is designed to remove your guilt. When David asked God to forgive him, he also asked God to *"restore to me the joy of Your salvation…"* (v. 12) because he recognized that a relationship with God is irreplaceable: *This joy that I have, the world didn't give it to me, and the world can't take it away!*

Perhaps you once enjoyed walking with the Lord, but your lifestyle has caused a separation in your relationship with God. If you're still reading this book at this point, you must have a desire to walk with Him again. The enemy might have convinced you that you're damaged goods, but that's the farthest thing from the truth! It doesn't matter what you've done or where you are in life; if you desire to return to God, He's waiting for you with open arms! Don't try to hide your sin behind excuses and lies. Be willing to confront your sin and accept the consequences. God is not only willing to rebuild you, but He wants to make you whole. Isaiah 64:8 says, *"God is the potter, and we are the clay...."* Allow Him to break, shape, make and mold you into what He would have you to be.

You might feel like an underachieving Christian, who just can't seem to get it together. Perhaps your church community has ostracized you because your sin was too big for you to be around them on Sunday mornings. You might even be on the verge of giving up because of how far you've fallen down. Well, the devil is a liar! Although you might have fallen down, you can get back up again in the Name of Jesus – It's time to come back home!

1 John 1:9 says, *"He is faithful and just to forgive us and cleanse us from all unrighteousness."* If you would like to rededicate your life to God, the following is a sample prayer of rededication:

Heavenly Father, I choose this day to rededicate my life to You. I commit my heart, my mind, my words, my actions, everything I have and everything that I am to You. I purposefully draw close to You, and I thank You that You draw close to me. I ask that You forgive me of my sins. Likewise, I release and forgive anyone who has sinned against me. Restore Your joy in my heart. I now receive Your love, instruction, comfort and guidance. Thank You for receiving me as Your own. Thank You for a fresh start with You. Now, Lord, use me for Your service. In Jesus' Name, Amen!

It really is that simple, and God really is that good! You are accepted by God! Rededication is simply the act of rededicating your life to God. It's a decision made by a Christian who has fallen away from the practices of Christianity but turns back to Christ and strives to follow Him more completely.

However, you cannot put the cart before the horse. You cannot rededicate your life to the Lord if you have not dedicated yourself to Him in the first place. This is accomplished by receiving and accepting Jesus Christ as your personal Lord and Savior. If you have never been born again, the following chapter is just for you!

Reflections

_____

_____

_____

_____

_____

_____

_____

_____

_____

_____

_____

_____

_____

_____

_____

_____

_____

Chapter 5

You Must Be Born Again!

While this book was written for the believer who struggles with sin, I would be remiss if I ended it without a roadmap to Christ for the nonbeliever. I ask this question nearly every Sunday morning at the conclusion of my sermons, and I'd like to pose it to you right now. This is probably the most important question of your life! In fact, your answer will determine your joy or sorrow for all eternity.

Here's the question: "Are You Saved?" If Jesus were to return today, are you absolutely sure you would go to Heaven? Now, let me be clear. This is not a question of whether or not you have good morals and values. I'm also not asking if you consider yourself to be a good person. Sadly enough, many good people will be turned away from the Lord on the Day of Judgment! Once again, the question is: "Are You Saved? Are You Born Again?"

John 3:1-7: *"There was a man of the Pharisees named Nicodemus, a ruler of the Jews. This man came to Jesus by night and said to Him, "Rabbi, we know that You are a teacher come from God;*

for no one can do these signs that You do unless God is with him." Jesus answered and said to him, "Most assuredly, I say to you, unless one is born again, he cannot see the kingdom of God." Nicodemus said to Him, "How can a man be born when he is old? Can he enter a second time into his mother's womb and be born?" Jesus answered, "Most assuredly, I say to you, unless one is born of water and the Spirit, he cannot enter the kingdom of God. That which is born of the flesh is flesh, and that which is born of the Spirit is spirit. Do not marvel that I said to you, 'You must be born again."

To comprehend the Biblical concept of being born again, it is necessary to understand that there are two kinds of births. The first birth is the physical birth when you were born into this world from your mother. When the Bible speaks of being born of water, it means this physical birth, not baptism. The second birth is a spiritual birth, which means to be born of God's Holy Spirit. By now, you might be confused and ask, "Why does a person need to be born spiritually?" Or, "What is a spiritual birth?" Rest assured that the word of God gives us the plan of how to be born again, which means to be saved. His plan is simple, and you can be saved today!

First, you must realize that you are a sinner. Romans 3:23 says, *"For all have sinned, and come short of the glory of God."* Because you are a sinner, you are condemned to death. Remember Romans 6:23: *"For the wages [payment] of sin is death."* This includes eternal separation from God in Hell. Lastly, Hebrews 9:27 says, *"…it is appointed unto men once to die, but after this the judgment."*

God loves us so much that He gave His only begotten Son to bear our sins and die in our place. 2 Corinthians 5:21 says, *"…He hath made Him [Jesus, Who knew no sin] to be sin for us, that we might be made the righteousness of God in Him."* Jesus had to shed His blood and die. Leviticus 17:11 says, *"For the life of the flesh is in the blood."* Also Hebrews 9:22: *"without shedding of blood is no remission [pardon]"* Finally, Romans 5:8: *"…God commended His love toward us, in that, while we were yet sinners, Christ died for us."*

In Acts 16:30-31, the Philippian jailer asked Paul and Silas, *"Sirs, what must I do to be saved?"* They responded, *"Believe on the Lord Jesus Christ, and you shall be saved."* This message is applicable to us today. Simply put, believe in Him as the One who bore your sin, died in your place and was buried and resurrected, then you will be saved. John 1:12 states, *"But as many as received Him, to them gave He power to become the sons of God, even to them that believe on His name."*

Romans 10:13 says, *"For whosoever shall call upon the name of the Lord shall be saved."* This includes you! Yet you must remember that God never forces anyone to accept Jesus as their Savior. The Lord will not muscle, burglarize or force His way into your life. He simply stands at the door of our hearts and offers a warm invitation to anyone who will accept the gift of Salvation.

John 3:16 tells us, *"For God so loved the world that He gave His only begotten Son, that whosoever believes in Him will not perish, but they will have everlasting life."* The gift of Salvation is free! You can't buy it; you can only accept and receive it! Romans 5:15 says, *"But the free gift is not like the offense. For if by the one man's offense many died, much more the grace of God and the gift by the grace of the one Man, Jesus Christ, abounded to many."*

Our Salvation was paid for by the precious blood of our

Lord and Savior Jesus Christ. All you have to do is step out on faith and receive Him as your Savior. You don't have to pass a background check, nor is there a probationary period. The only requirement is that you believe in Jesus and receive Him as your Savior! You can't save yourself! Take God at His word, and claim His salvation by faith. Believe, and you will be saved!

If you would like to invite Jesus into your heart and become saved, simply pray and believe this prayer of Salvation:

Oh God, I know I am a sinner. Please forgive me for my sins. I believe in Jesus! I believe that You lived, I believe that You died, I believe that You were raised from the grave after three days, and I believe that You will return one day to carry Your children home. Lord, I invite You into my heart and receive You as my Savior. Thank You for forgiving me for my sins, the gift of salvation and everlasting life. Now, Lord, live Your life through me. In Jesus' Name, Amen!

What Now?
Continue in the will of God by:

1. Praying on a regular basis.
2. Reading your Bible on a regular basis.
3. Attending a church that teaches the word of God.
4. Telling others about the Gospel of Jesus Christ.

<u>Come As You Are</u>

I shook my head in disbelief. This couldn't be the right place. After all, I couldn't possibly be welcome here. I had been given an invitation several times, by several different people, and had finally decided to see what this place was all about. But, this just couldn't be the right place.

Quickly, I glanced down at the invitation that I clutched in my hand. I scanned past the words, "Come as you are, No jacket required" and found the location. Yes, I was at the right place. I peered through the window again and saw a room of people whose faces seemed to glow with joy. All were neatly dressed, adorned in fine garments and appeared strangely clean as they dined at this exquisite restaurant.

Ashamed, I looked down at my own tattered and torn clothing, covered in stains. I was dirty, in fact, filthy. A foul smell seemed to consume me and I couldn't shake the grime that clung to my body. As I turned around to leave, the words from the invitation seemed to leap out at me, "Come as you are. No jacket required."

I decided to give it a shot. Mustering up every bit of courage I could find, I opened the door to this restaurant and walked up to a man standing behind a podium.

"Your name, sir?" he asked me with a smile.

"Jimmy D. Brown," I mumbled without looking up. I thrust my hands deep into my pockets, hoping to conceal their stains.

He didn't seem to notice the filth that I was covered in and he continued, "Very good, sir. A table is reserved in your name. Would you like to be seated?"

I couldn't believe what I heard! A grin broke out on my face and I said, "Yes, of course!"

He led me to a table and sure enough, there was a placard with my name written on it in a deep, dark blood red color.

As I browsed over a menu, I saw many delightful items listed. There were things like: peace, joy, blessings, confidence, assurance, hope, love, faith and mercy. I realized that this was no ordinary restaurant! I flipped the menu back to the front in order to see where I was at: "God's Grace" was the name of this place!

The man returned and said, "I recommend the 'Special of the Day.' With it, you are entitled to heaping portions of everything on this menu."

You've got to be kidding, I thought to myself. You mean I can have ALL of this? "What is the Special of the Day?" I asked with excitement ringing in my voice.

"Salvation," was his reply.

"I'll take it," I practically cried out.

Then, as quickly as I made that statement, the joy left my body. A sick, painful ache jerked through my stomach and tears filled my eyes.

Between my sobs I said, "Mister, look at me. I'm dirty and

nasty. I'm unclean and unworthy of such things. I'd love to have all of this, but, I just can't afford it."

Undaunted, the man smiled again. "Sir, your check has already been taken care of by that Gentleman over there." He pointed to a man at the front of the room. "His Name is Jesus!"

Turning, I saw a man whose very presence seemed to light the room. He was almost too much to look at. I found myself walking towards Him and in a shaking voice I whispered, "Sir, I'll wash the dishes or sweep the floors or take out the trash. I'll do anything I can do to repay you for all of this."

He opened His arms and said with a smile, "Son, all of this is yours if you just come unto me. Ask me to clean you up and I will. Ask me to take away the stains and it is done. Ask me to allow you to feast at my table and you will eat. Remember, the table is reserved in your name. The only thing you have to do is accept this gift that I offer you."

Astonished, I fell at his feet and said, "Please, Jesus. Please clean up my life. Please change me and sit me at your table and give me this new life."

Immediately, I heard the words, "It is finished."

I looked down and white robes adorned my squeaky clean body. Something strange and wonderful had happened. I felt new, like a weight had been lifted and I found myself seated at His table.

He then said to me, "The Special of the Day has been served. Salvation is yours."

We sat and talked for a great while and I so enjoyed the time that I spent with Him. He told me, me of all people, that He would like for me to come back as often as I liked for another helping from God's Grace. He made it clear that He wanted me to spend as much time with Him as possible.

As it drew near time for me to go back outside into the real world, He whispered to me softly, "And Lo, I am with you always."

And then, He said something to me that I will never forget. He said, "My child, do you see these empty tables throughout this room?"

"Yes Lord, I see them. What do they mean?" I replied.

"These are reserved tables, but the individuals whose names are on each placard have not accepted their invitations to dine. Would you be so kind as to hand out these invitations to those who have not joined us yet?" Jesus asked.

"Of course," I said with excitement as I picked up the invitations.

As I turned to leave He said, "Go ye therefore into all nations."

I walked into God's Grace dirty and hungry, stained in sin. My righteousness as filthy rags. And Jesus cleaned me up. But I walked out a brand new man; robed in white, justified by His righteousness.

And so, I'll keep my promise to my Lord. I'll go. I'll spread the

Word. I'll share the Gospel. I'll hand out the invitations… starting with you.

Have you been to God's Grace? There's a table reserved in your name, and here's your invitation – Come As You Are. No Jacket Required.

AUTHOR UNKNOWN

"For by grace you have been saved through faith, and that not of yourselves; it is the gift of God, not of works, lest anyone should boast."---Ephesians 2:8-9

Reflections

_____

_____

_____

_____

_____

_____

_____

_____

_____

_____

_____

_____

_____

_____

_____

Epilogue:
Be Encouraged

"Therefore we also, since we are surrounded by so great a cloud of witnesses, let us lay aside every weight, and the sin which so easily ensnares us, and let us run with endurance the race that is set before us, looking unto Jesus, the author and finisher of our faith, who for the joy that was set before Him endured the cross, despising the shame, and has sat down at the right hand of the throne of God." Hebrews 12:1-2

In the life of every individual, there is a "besetting" sin that can tower like a mountain between the individual and God. This is, *the sin which so easily ensnares us,* and it differs according to the person. In other words, what is a besetting sin to one person may not trouble another person at all. Sometimes this sin will be quite obvious to others. But in other cases, it will be hidden in the heart and known only to that individual and God. In either case, it is harassing and perplexing, and if it's not addressed; will linger and grow, usually ending in a tragic moral failure.

Practically every believer wrestles with a habitually assaulting sin, even those whose service to Christ is of outstanding quality. Moses, with his explosive temper. David, with his weakness for women. These were devoted men of God who walked humbly in the will of God, but when they grew weak and weary in faith, their besetting sin reared up its ugly head to challenge them. Fortunately, both Moses and David realized the need to run to God, and when they fell, they cried out for His help. When it comes to a besetting sin: it will either drive us closer to God, if we run to Him for help when we need it, or it will drive us away from Him, if we yield to its desires.

As believers, when we accept Jesus Christ into our heart: there should be a change of mind, a change of heart and a change of direction in our lives. There should be a strong conviction within our spirit when we attempt to do the things we used to do: The explicit lyrics to a secular song makes our ears bleed. The alcoholic beverage of choice that caused us to make bad decisions just doesn't taste right anymore. The dirty jokes being told around the water cooler at work now makes us feel uncomfortable.

Don't become defeated by your sin problem. You're not "stuck" in your sins. Unfortunately, many people have given up the hope of ever changing; leaving them feeling alone, ashamed and frustrated by their sin problem. As well, there are others who might feel like sin is no big deal, since God is going to forgive them anyway – this is a very dangerous position to take.

The gospel of grace, when properly understood, should not steer an individual to licentiousness (unrestrained by law or general morality) but to righteousness. While Jesus fully and freely forgives us, he also instructs us in John 8:11: *"Go now and leave your life of sin!"*

As accustomed to Paul's style, he anticipates a question and addresses it before his critics can complain. He used a similar technique in Romans 3:5: *"But if our righteousness brings out God's righteousness more clearly, what shall we say? That God is unjust in bringing his wrath on us?"*

In order to understand why he raises this issue, we need to go back to Romans 5:20: *"Moreover the law entered that the offense might abound. But where sin abounded, grace abounded much more."* This statement would cause many people to say, "If we receive more grace when we sin, then why not just sin some more?" Read Paul's rebuttal in Romans 6:1-7:

"What shall we say, then? Shall we go on sinning so that grace may increase? By no means! We died to sin; how can we live in it any longer? Or don't you know that all of us who were baptized into Christ Jesus were baptized into His death? We were therefore buried with Him through baptism into death in order that, just as Christ was raised from the dead through the glory of the Father, we too may live a new life. If we have been united with Him like this in His death, we will certainly also be united with Him in His resurrection. For we know that our old self was crucified with Him so that the body of sin might be done away with, that we should no longer be slaves to sin because anyone who has died has been freed from sin."

The phrase "go on sinning" means to stay in sin. These words were used of one who remained in the same place for a long time, a habitual routine. However, we can't continue in sin until our heart's content, doing so becomes an exploitation of the grace of God.

It would be helpful at this point to understand the word antinomianism. The phrase "anti" means against and "nomos" is the word for law. An antinomian is the person who says, "I'm saved but I can sin any way I want because God will forgive me regardless of how I live." You need to understand, this is not biblical Christianity.

Justification was not extended to give us a license to sin, but as liberation from sin. Thus, if you carry on in the same manner that you did when you were in the world, your actions are speaking louder than your words. When you become born again, you lose your desires to do anything that is contrary to the will of God. You will miss the mark on occasion, but you become motivated to go in a different direction: with new interests, new desires, a new walk and a new talk. An unchanged life is the mark of an unchanged heart. Salvation is more than a just a transaction; it is a transformation.

There is a reality that we must all face, and that is: no matter who you are today, no matter how well of a Christian life you're living today, there's somebody out there who knew you before you knew the Lord! They knew you before you started attending church on a regular basis. They knew you before you started studying your bible and entertaining an active prayer life. They knew you in your "B.C." days (Before Christ) when you were making bad decisions because there was no accountability.

Those who knew you back when may not respond to your new life the way you would expect. Many of your associates will take a wait and see attitude, and observe you from a distance. They will listen to your conversations and monitor your movements, just to see if this new life in Christ is for real. Don't be surprised if someone from your past challenges your new life because it threatens their own.

Your life has become transparent now. You may very well be the only Bible that many of your family, friends and associates will ever read. This truth becomes a living testimony, because the person in whom they used to know has literally died. You are a new creature who's been washed in the blood of the Lamb. Again, Romans 6:6 says, *"knowing this, that our old man was crucified with Him, that the body of sin might be done away with, that we should no longer be slaves of sin."*

The phrase "done away with" literally means "rendered powerless." The whole goal here is freedom from sin. Jesus said in John 8:36: *"So if the Son sets you free, you will be free indeed."* You can do it! You can live for Christ!

Finally, the story is told how recently at a fund-raising banquet for a school for children with special needs, one of the fathers got up and told a story about his son named Shéa. He described how he and his son had been walking through the neighborhood of Brooklyn a week before, and they stopped to watch a group of boys playing baseball. Shéa does not communicate well, but he let his father know in his own way that he so wanted to play baseball with these boys.

The father thinks that there's no chance of this happening but he goes up to the pitcher and explains the situation. The pitcher makes an executive decision and says, "You know, it's the eighth inning. We're down by six. What have we got to lose? Come on in, we'll let you bat in the bottom of the ninth." Shéa is ecstatic.

But when the ninth inning comes things have turned around. Now they're down only by three runs and the bases are loaded. If they get a home run, they'll win the game. And now it's Shéa's turn to bat. The father's heart begins to beat rapidly as he wonders if they'll keep their promise to Shéa and let him bat. The team realizes their predicament so they have a little huddle. Then, to the father's amazement, they say to Shéa, "Come on. You're up to bat." And Shéa is absolutely delighted. He clutches the bat at a strange angle and holds it tightly.

Then the pitcher from the opposite team does an amazing thing. He takes several steps forward and lobs an easy one right over the plate. Shéa swings wildly and misses widely. Then a player from Shéa's team comes up behind him and gently wraps his arms around him. Together, they hold the bat. The pitcher lobs another one, and they bunt it, and the ball just rolls to the feet of the pitcher.

It's an easy out, but everybody's screaming: "Run to first. Run to first, Shéa!" And the pitcher throws it far and wide. Shéa makes first, and they say, "Run to second, Shéa! Run to second!" The guy out in the field is planning to whip it into second, but then realizes what is going on and throws it far and wide. Everyone starts yelling, "Run to third! Run to third!"

All the other players have crossed home plate and they start yelling, "Run home, Shéa! Take it home!" And just as he hits home plate the ball zings in. A loud uproar from both teams erupts; they put Shéa on their shoulders and parade him as a hero. (Source: "Preaching Today" Issue #285)

Friends, because of our sins we have all struck out spiritually.

But Jesus has wrapped His arms around us so that what He has experienced we have too. He's hit it out of the park in order to bring us safely home. In the meantime we enjoy the victory that He has won.

There is no joy, better than the one achieved when operating in the will of God! This truth encourages us to walk with Lord and remain in His will, knowing that by doing so; we are walking in faith and truly abiding in Him. Faith is the "substance" that is necessary to produce the "miraculous" in our lives! Through faith, we can achieve the unachievable, accomplish the impossible and reach the unreachable! When we put our trust in the Lord, we don't have to worry about the frustrating turns that the roads of life may bring, because we're walking by faith, knowing that the Lord will always make a way!

Be Encouraged!

Reflections

_____

_____

_____

_____

_____

_____

_____

_____

_____

_____

_____

_____

_____

_____

_____

If you've been blessed by this book,
I would love to hear your story.
As well, I welcome your comments:

ronkelly7@gmail.com

For Booking and Speaking Engagements:

Ron Kelly
P.O. Box 995
Lee's Summit, MO 64063

816-623-9900

Purchase additional copies of this book
at your local bookstore.

or visit:

http://bookstore.authorhouse.com

www.OopsRonKelly.com

Stay Connected w/ Ron Kelly:

www.OopsRonKelly.com

Linkedin

Twitter: @ronkelly7

http://youtube.com/ronkelly7

http://facebook.com/ronkelly7

https://vimeo.com/ronkelly